Serving up Retirement

for the food & beverage industry

Guest Check

453272

Buy a house

Kids college

TAX-FREE
Retirement!!

Thank You - Call Again

GUEST RECEIPT

453272

Larry P. Stidman

Foreword: Christopher Westbrook

Serving Up Retirement for the Food and Beverage Industry

Editor, Christopher Carson
Foreword by Christopher Westbrook
Cover design by Nina Garibay

For bulk purchases, contact:
info@CompleteBenefitSolutionsLLC.com

Retirement Preservation Institute
Printed in the United States of America

CONTENTS

DEDICATION

This book is dedicated to all individuals in the food & beverage industry who want to build retirement wealth without worrying about what happens when the stock market crashes like it did from late 2007 to early 2009 (-59%).

ACKNOWLEDGEMENTS

As with all books that cover financial planning and wealth building concepts, this one required help and input from many people and sources.

Always at the top of my list are my amazing wife, Kristin, and our three wonderful children, Landon, Erik & Sophia. They are truly my inspiration in life.

Special thanks goes to Chris Carson for encouraging me to write this book and for publishing it.

To my staff - thank you for your hard work, commitment and valuable contributions to this enterprise every single day.

To my parents, family and friends, I owe my deepest thanks for allowing me to be me and for being who you are.

FOREWORD

Most restaurant owners and partners need to start or catch up on their retirement. As one of them, you know that you have spent a lot of money, hard work, and time building your successful business, but you also need to watch the future and have a complete *exit strategy*. You need control of your money and you need it to grow, not decline. You need to be able to access it along the way in an emergency or opportunity, to draw additional money if you want to keep working, and to draw it forever if you want or need to truly retire.

In this book, you will learn about two powerful retirement preservation and wealth-building tools. The general features of them are that:

1. They do not let your account balance decline when the stock market drops and

2. They lock in your gains when the market goes up.

In addition, one tool guarantees you an 8% rate of return (accumulation value) combined with a lifetime income guarantee.

Most securities-licensed advisors (stock brokers) will tell you that you need an "allocated group of stocks, bonds and mutual funds" for long-term growth and a CD for short-term growth. If you had taken that advice in 2007, the chances are significant that in 2009 your account value would have been 50% of where you started.

The majority of stock brokers and bankers *do not* disclose to their clients that they can't discuss and certainly can't sell the retirement preservation and wealth building tools I discuss in this book (ones that protect your principal and locks in gains). If they did disclose these facts, then individuals would never hire them to manage their money.

My point is that, with our team's knowledge of the wealth-building tools in the marketplace coupled with the fact of being an insider in the financial services industry, we are in a very unique position to present this book giving readers the "real story" when it comes to viable wealth-building tools.

I hope you enjoy reading the book as much as I have enjoyed helping put it together. As you will see throughout the book, if you have any questions, feel free to contact us at www.CompleteBenefitSolutionsLLC.com for more information.

Christopher Westbrook
Complete Benefit Solutions, LLC.

PREFACE

My guess is that everyone has been shown a way to "get rich quick" or get rich "without risk or worries." You have probably attended a seminar that was supposed to teach you the "secrets" wealthy people use to become wealthy.

For some reason, most people believe that successful individuals have knowledge of "secret" wealth-building tools that everyday people do not have.

Over the last 17 years in the financial industry, I have seen a lot of "magic-pill" plans spring up. As a financial professional, it is my job to research, form an opinion and educate my clients on old and new retirement and wealth-building tools.

While I'd like to tell you that I have some "secret" plan to help build your wealth in ways that no one else knows; that is not the case. No such plan exists (no matter what your bank, your stock broker or some talking head on television has been telling you). You will find in this book something new to most readers— insight into alternative ways of *Retirement Preservation*.

The tools shown are widely known by financial planners, CPAs and life insurance advisors. However, most of them do *not* understand their power and protective features which make them excellent wealth-building tools for many individuals.

My goal with this book is very simple. I want to educate you on these tools so that you will understand specifically how one or more of them may be useful in a plan to help you with *Retirement Preservation*.

So that we can discuss these tools in more detail, I am including my personal email address

Larry@CompleteBenefitSolutionsLLC.com

and my direct office phone number

501-622-2552.

Please do not hesitate to contact me.

DEFINITION
OF
RETIREMENT PRESERVATION

Retirement Preservation: a substantial amount of money is positioned in wealth-building tools that will not decrease in value if the stock market goes down.

For example, between late 2007 and early 2009, the market fell by more than half. For many people, their accounts declined dramatically. The time left for them to recoup that money may not exist for older individuals. Furthermore, their accounts now have to *double* just to catch up to where they were before the decline.

Another wealth-building tool that will not decrease in value if the stock market goes down is a guaranteed rate of return (accumulation value) combined with a lifetime income that you can never outlive!

As you can see, my definition of retirement preservation is different from the definition of most financial industry advisors.

Here are a few different ways that people *attempt* to preserve their retirement funds:

1. Position funds in conservative certificate of deposits (CDs). Money is CDs are virtually risk free. However, they provide pathetically *low yields* and *taxable income* every year.

2. Acquire real estate (rental or investment). Real estate over time is usually not a bad investment. However, real estate values can plummet for many reasons and there is *no guaranteed income*.

3. Bonds have proven over time to be a conservative wealth-building tool. However, *bond returns and/ or income are not guaranteed,* and the average returns have not been very good.

4. Stocks and mutual funds. Actually, these should not be on this list, but millions of individuals are directed to buy a "proper mix" of stocks and mutual funds to create and maintain a retirement nest egg. As we all know, individuals that had some, or unfortunately a majority, of their retirement savings in stocks and mutual funds lost 50%+ from late 2007 to early 2009.

SUMMARY

The two tools discussed in this book can be purchased from financially secure insurance companies. Because of their product designs, *your retirement savings will be protected from downturns* in the stock market.

The first tool discussed will allow your money to grow tax-free and can be removed tax-free during retirement.

The second tool will have a guaranteed rate of return (accumulation value) that will pay you a guaranteed income for life.

These features meet my definition of "Retirement Preservation."

Will the tools discussed provide you a 100% risk free path to retirement? No. There is no such retirement or wealth building platform. The key to building your retirement nest egg is to work with advisors who know what they are dong and can help guide you in the best financial tools to build your wealth at companies that will stand the test of time.

1

RESTAURANT RETIREMENT

The premise of this book for restaurant owners sets out a new way to look at retirement, not just as an exit plan but as an operating tool with other benefits.

If you fail to plan, you plan to fail.

Whether you've just started out, are already running a successful restaurant, or are struggling to get by, an exit plan is a must. We'll highlight the traditional plans briefly and move on to the new ideas that are far easier to use, more flexible and less costly. In fact, we want to move to a tax-free retirement plan where possible.

Most restaurant owners and partners like you need to start or to catch up on their retirement. You have spent a lot of money, hard work, and time building your business, but you also need to watch the future and have a complete exit strategy. You need control of your money and you need it to grow, not decline. You need to be able to access it along the way in an emergency or opportunity, to keep working while drawing money if you want to keep working, to draw it forever if you need to truly retire.

You should be making arrangements also for some sort of retirement plan for your full and even part-time employees if you are not already providing them with this benefit. You can do this without cost to your company or to yourself!

What are some benefits of a plan for employees? Loyalty and long-term employment. National studies have shown employee turnover is far lower. With the cost in time and money of training new employees, the long-term savings can be significant. Attract and retain higher quality employees by offering retirement benefits for a competitive edge over other restaurants that offer no such benefits. We will show you how to do this without cost to yourself or the company.

Why retirement benefits to your *part-time* employees? Your old trained, reliable workers and their friends will be eager to return to your restaurant whenever you require extra help. Your industry relies heavily on part-time employees, and the benefits can be provided at no cost to you or the business. But first the traditonal plans (which have been unwieldy, confusing and sometimes expensive). These plans include:

SEPs

Simplified employee pensions are generic retirement plans that allow you to contribute and deduct up to 20% of self-employment income (25% of salary if you're an employee of your own corporation). SEPs are much simpler to establish and administer than Keogh profit-sharing and pension plans. No annual government reports are required. Ongoing administrative expenses are minimal.

Keogh Plans

Keogh plans are the self-employed equivalent of corporate retirement programs, either profit-sharing plans or defined benefit pension plans subject to a $49,000 ceiling for a targeted annual retirement and you're locked into making the contribution each year.

Solo 401(k)

You can contribute up to 100% of the first $16,500 of your 2010 compensation or self-employment income ($22,000 if you'll be 50 or older at year-end).

Roth IRAs

When you still want or need more retirement tax breaks. You pay tax now and fund the Roth IRA. Limits exist on contributons. A Roth IRA may save more taxes in the long run.

If You Have Employees...

If your business has employees, a SEP, Solo 401(k) or Keogh generally must cover them as well — you'll probably have to make contributions that don't just benefit yourself. One carrier will do a free review under the new and current tax laws to get you more benefits and less risk, fewer fees and simpler administration. Contact us for more information.

What You Really Want

Something:

- simple,
- flexible,
- tax-free,
- good growth,
- no risk,
- access to capital,
- no fees,
- availability of assets prior to age 59 with no penalty.

Keep reading.

2

"OLD-FASHIONED" RETIREMENT WEALTH BUILDING

Nothing is wrong with building your retirement wealth the *old-fashioned way* through stocks and mutual funds.

However, most of today's workforce knows that these old-fashioned ways have not worked too well over the last 10 years.

The consequence of having significant amounts of money in the stock market during this time frame has devastated most retirement plans.

- Between 2000 & 2002, the market lost 46% of its value!

- Between 2007 & 2009, the market last 59% from its highest point to its lowest point.

Making matters worse, most people invest in mutual funds. Even when the market goes down, the mutual funds incur *account maintenance charges* that *increase losses*.

Another common expense of the old-fashioned way of retirement wealth building is *stock broker fees*. When you add the market losses to all the fees and expenses, it's no wonder that most workers lost more than two-thirds of their retirement nest egg between 2007 and 2009.

Due to the poor advice given to the American worker on how to grow a retirement nest egg, many have had to put off retirement (or even go back to work if they were already retired). Many people have had to reassess how they are going to pay for their kids' college. The retirement preservation tools discussed in this book can help ease or even satisfy these concerns.

RECOVERING FROM MARKET LOSSES

If the stock market decreases by 15% in a year, how much does the market have to go up next year to get the account back to even? Most individuals will say 15%. It sort of makes sense that whatever it goes down this year; it must go up by the same next year to break even.

The problem with this math is that you now have less money invested; and therefore, you need a greater return on your money the following year to get back to breakeven. The following chart illustrates the gain needed to recover from different losses:

Traditional Investing	
Amount of Loss	% Gain Needed to Recover the Following Year
10%	11%
20%	25%
30%	43%
40%	67%
50%	100%

TAX DEFERRED INVESTING INTO 401(K) PLANS AND IRAS

Banks, stock brokers and the federal government have done a good job promoting the idea of planning for your retirement by using a tax-deferred vehicle such as 401(k)s and IRAs. While these can be nice investment tools to build your retirement nest egg, you still need to strategically think before putting your money into these types of tax-deferred vehicles.

Contrary to what you have been repeatedly told by bankers, stock brokers, and the talking heads on TV and radio programs, *tax-deferred vehicles are not "tax favorable"*, but instead they are "tax-hostile" because *all* of the money that comes out of a qualified plan or IRA is income-taxed at your current income tax bracket.

- Because income taxes are currently near an all-time *low*, it is a high probability that income tax rates will be higher when you retire.

- You cannot access the money in a tax-deferred vehicle until after the age of 59½ without substantial tax penalties.

Most working Americans are scared and are wondering where in the world they are supposed to position their money for growth so that they can retire at some point in the future.

WHAT TO DO?

Let's discuss *two alternative strategies* that keep your money from going backwards when the market goes down and locks in your gains when the market goes up.

TAX-FREE RETIREMENT NEST EGG

One of the retirement preservation tools detailed in this book is the proper use of an *Equity Indexed Universal Life* (EIUL) insurance policy. A properly designed EIUL can be one of if not the "best" tax-favored and protective retirement building and preservation tools available.

If an individual knew how tax-favorable and protective a properly designed EIUL insurance policy can be and how such a policy can outperform tax-deferred 401(k) plans and significantly outperform the use of a post-tax brokerage account to build wealth, he would go out of his way to sit down with a knowledgeable and properly trained life insurance advisor.

DID YOU KNOW?

- Cash inside a properly designed EIUL insurance policy is allowed to grow tax free and come out tax free.

- Some policies tie their growth to the S&P 500 stock index.

- There are polices that have 100% principal protection on the cash value, and the cash will not decrease due to negative market performance.

- There is a policy that currently credits 180% of what the blended indexes return.

- Some polices come with high early cash surrender values.

- Some policies included a free long-term care benefit.

Again, because the cash in the policy is allowed to grow tax-free and be removed tax-free in an EIUL insurance policy, it stands out as one of the main reasons to use it as a retirement building and preservation tool.

When an individual is sold a properly designed EUIL, the sale, in large part, usually revolves around "loans" that can be taken from the policy "income tax free."

You will pay no income tax if you borrow cash value from your life insurance policy.

You do not receive income from a life insurance policy; instead, you *access the cash via loans*. This can give you virtually unlimited access to your cash value on a tax-advantaged basis. Also, these loans do not need to be paid back, as the loan is repaid at death through a reduction in the death benefit. These loans can be set up for regular disbursement, started and stopped or used just as needed.

The cash value built up in an EIUL insurance policy can be borrowed systematically to help supplement your retirement income, pay for college expenses for your loved ones, or for any other purpose.

TWO POINTS TO EMPHASIZE WITH THESE WITHDRAWALS:

- The funds are tax-free and

- you do *not* have to wait until you are 59½ to access the funds.

ANOTHER VALUABLE ATTRIBUTE

Using life insurance as a retirement wealth-building and preservation tool makes sense because life insurance is "self-completing."

One of three things will happen to you after purchasing a life insurance policy:

- You can live,

- you can die or

- you can suffer a disability.

A properly structured life insurance policy can provide for you no matter which of these events occurs. Either you or your beneficiaries will receive funds from the policy — thus the policy "self-completes."

With all the favorable points mentioned above, you need to guard against taking too much cash out of your policy through loans. When an insured borrows cash from a life insurance policy, the policy must stay in place until death. Otherwise, the insured will have to pay taxes on the loans received that exceed the premium paid.

IF YOU ARE NOT HEALTHY

Since this strategy utilizes a life insurance policy, what happens if you are not healthy or have marginal health? If you or your spouse are not healthy, using life insurance as a retirement building tool becomes much more challenging. The cost of insurance annually inside the policy will significantly affect how much cash you will build and be able to borrow from the policy. However, even if the insured is rated up because of health, the amount of cash available at retirement is still higher than most tax-deferred investments and brokerage accounts.

EXAMPLE:

The chart on the next page illustrates an EIUL policy with other tax-deferred and tax-hostile financial tools.

A 35 year old male in good health contributes $6,000 per year into an EIUL insurance policy for ten years.

At age 65, he will begin to borrow "tax-free" from his policy.

The amount of annual "tax-free" withdrawals is $28,200 through age 100.

Notice that all other instruments, the CD, the Money Market fund, the taxable bonds, the IRA and 401(k), have long since run out of money, but the EIUL still has both cash value and substantial death benefits.

All of the other financial tools run out of money between the age of 70 and 75. Unless you do not want to live past age 70, none of the alternative tools presented will meet your retirement needs.

THE POWER OF RETIREMENT PRESERVATION

➤ $60,000 total contributions made

➤ 35 year old contributes $6,000 annually ($500 monthly) for 10 years

➤ Compare the power of Retirement Preservation™ to four other financial alternatives

➤ At age 65, Retirement Preservation™ income begins TAX FREE until age 85

➤ AFTER TAX income from other financial alternatives

| Age | Income Amount | After Tax Values (annual yields) | | | | Retirement Preservation™ | |
		Certificate of Deposit 5.5%	Money Market 7.5%	Taxable Bonds 8.0%	IRA or 401(k) 6.0%	Cash Surrender Value	Death Benefit
65	28,200	146,948	229,226	255,093	247,620	387,857	561,753
66	28,200	123,467	212,334	240,507	225,112	390,393	564,289
67	28,200	99,385	194,492	225,045	201,254	393,031	566,927
68	28,200	74,121	175,646	208,656	175,964	395,759	569,655
69	28,200	47,815	155,739	191,283	149,157	398,586	572,482
70	28,200	20,424	134,714	172,868	120,741	401,499	575,395
80	28,200	(323,990)	(152,909)	(84,420)	(276,271)	432,695	606,791
90	28,200	(839,969)	(650,063)	(545,184)	(987,260)	415,694	589,590
100	28,200	(1,612,974)	(1,509,399)	(1,370,342)	(2,260,532)	73,754	247,650

Retirement Preservation™ performance based on 15% annual point-to-point cap, 100% participation rate, and based on an 8.61% annual rate of return. Rate of return is based on a 20 year average of the S&P 500 (1987-2007) with a maximum annual point-to-point cap of 15%.

ANOTHER EXAMPLE:

Using the same parameters as the previous example, let's compare how much money could be withdrawn from our Retirement Preservation platform and the same alternative financial tools for 20 years (age 65 - 85).

THE POWER OF
RETIREMENT PRESERVATION™

> $60,000 total contributions made
> 35 year old contributes $6,000 annually ($500 monthly) for 10 years
> Compare the power of Retirement Preservation™ to four other financial alternatives
> At age 65, Retirement Preservation™ income begins TAX FREE until age 85
> AFTER TAX income from other financial alternatives

Retirement Preservation EIUL Platform *TAX-FREE Withdrawals*	$34,700
Certificate of Deposit	$6,220
Money Market	$11,256
Taxable Bonds	$12,971
IRA or 401(k)	$10,892

Notice that none of the alternative financial tools have an annual withdrawal amount anywhere close to what could be removed from the Retirement Preservation platform via tax-free policy loans using conservative assumptions.

Which instrument generates the most money for your retirement? The bottom line with comparisons between funding tax-hostile financial tools vs. an EIUL policy is that there is no comparison.

CONCLUSION ON
THE POWER OF USING EIULS FOR RETIREMENT PRESERVATION

If you like the possibility of earning upwards of 10-15% return, would like to allow your cash to grow tax-free and be removed tax-free, and would like to avoid the stock market's negative years with a 1-3% minimum guarantee, then you should consider using an EIUL for retirement wealth-building and preservation.

In addition, an EIUL policy protects you from yourself because the built-in guarantees eliminate the need to panic sell during periods of market declines.

I hope this chapter has helped you understand the tax-free characteristics of building retirement wealth in a properly designed EIUL policy.

I imagine that many readers will learn that the last life insurance policy that they purchased was not fully explained to them, or was simply not the best product for their specific situation. If you fall into this category, do not hesitate to email me at Larry@CompleteBenefitSolutionsLLC.com; and I'd be happy to review your current policy to see if we can fix it or 1035 (tax-free) exchange it to a policy that better meets your needs.

4

FIXED INDEXED ANNUITIES

After reading the previous chapter, you may feel that a properly designed Equity Indexed Universal Life (EIUL) insurance policy might be the most protective and tax-favorable retirement building tool available. However, if you are over the age of 60, it is going to be difficult to make an EIUL work as the best method.

Regardless of your age, *principal protection* is one of the most important aspects of retirement wealth building and preservation. Generally speaking, when the average investor thinks of building wealth tools that preserve principal, they typically think of low-earning tools such as:

- Certificates of deposits (CD),

- money market accounts, and sometimes

- fixed annuities.

All three of these guarantee that your money will not decrease, but the growth rate is usually very low, and CDs and money market accounts create annually taxable income.

A hybrid-concept tool for retirement wealth building and preservation is a *Fixed Indexed Annuity* (FIA). Making FIAs an attractive retirement wealth building tool are two key features:

- FIAs (like the three tools mentioned above) guarantee *your money will never decrease* due to a downturn in the stock market.

- FIAs *lock in your gains every year*, converting it to principal and thus protecting it from decreasing.

FIAs can also be used to *guarantee a certain rate of return* coupled with a *guaranteed income for life* that you can never outlive. Also, some FIAs include *free* long-term care benefits.

Does a retirement wealth building tool with the above mentioned traits interest you? Unfortunately, the majority of stock brokers and bankers do not use FIAs to help their clients preserve their retirement, and, therefore, stock market decreases take a heavy toll on most investors.

WHAT IS A FIXED INDEXED ANNUITY (FIA)?

An annuity is a contract between a buyer (typically an individual) and the issuer (typically an insurance company), whereby the contract owner agrees to pay the issuer an initial lump sum premium or payments over a period of time (flexible premium), during which the issuer guarantees the owner a stated minimum rate of return or the opportunity to participate in the growth of a market index.

The annuity contract is usually referred to as a policy because it is issued by an insurance company, and the owner is usually referred to as the policyholder.

As the name implies, a "fixed" indexed annuity is equipped with guarantees that variable annuities are not, such as a minimum earning rate if held for the contractual term. The bottom line with these guarantees is that the principal will *never decrease* due to negative stock market returns.

The "indexed" part of the name indicates that the *gains are linked to a particular stock index*. The Standard & Poor's 500 (S&P 500) stock index is the primary stock index used since the inception of FIAs over ten years ago.

Here is an example of how a FIA would have performed over a 5 year period with returns of 13%, -20%, 8%, -16% and 23% where the initial investment is $100,000.

	$100,000	$100,000
Year	Invested in S&P 500	Invested in a FIA
1	$113,000	$112,000
2	$90,400	$112,000
3	$97,632	$120,000
4	$82,011	$120,960
5	$100,871	$135,475

As you can see, when the market decreases, so does the account value invested in the S&P 500 stock index. However, in those negative years, the FIA flat-lined and retained its principal value. Also, in some of the positive years, the S&P 500 investment grew more than the FIA account. That is because most FIAs have a *cap* on the upside growth, and in this example, the cap was 12%.

To emphasize the protective features of FIAs, most advisors use a common phrase of "zero is your hero." This phrase literally means that you earn "zero" when the market declines; therefore, protecting your principal balance from market losses.

The following chart compares a $100,000 investment in a very volatile market that has an average return of zero over a 10-year period.

Why did the FIA end up with an account balance of $48,000 higher? Simply stated – the FIA returned *zero* instead of negative in down years, and returned up to the 8% cap in positive years. This is another great example of "zero is your hero."

FIAs are not the perfect retirement wealth-building and preservation tool for everyone, but based on their protective features, it is easy for a large percentage of individuals to justify allocating a portion of their retirement nest egg into these products.

FIAs are the only retirement wealth-building financial vehicle that offers all of the following benefits:

	S&P 500				FIA			
	Initial Value	Annual Yield		Year End Value	Initial Value	Annual Yield		Year End Value
Year		%	$			%	$	
1	$100,000	15%	$15,000	$115,000	$100,000	8%	$8,000	$108,000
2	$115,00	-8%	($9,200)	$105,800	$108,000	0%	$0	$108,00
3	$105,800	6%	$6,348	$112,548	$108,000	6%	$6,480	$114,480
4	$112,148	-10%	($11,215)	$100,913$	$114,480	0%	$0	$114,480
5	$100,933	9%	$9,084	$110,017	$114,480	8%	$9,158	$123,688
6	$110,017	-13%	($14,302)	$95,715	$123,688	0%	$0	$123,688
7	$95,715	15%	$10,529	$105,244	$123,688	8%	$2,591	$132,529
8	$106,244	-3%	($3,187)	$103,656	$132,529	0%	$0	$132,529
9	$103,056	7%	$7,214	$110,270	$132,529	7%	$9,347	$142,877
10	$110,270	-14%	($15,438)	$94,832	$142,877	0%	$0	$142,877
	Average Annual return of 0.00%				Average Annual Return of 2.70			

- 100% principal protection
- No up-front sales fees
- Opportunity to earn a guaranteed rate of return (accumulation value)
- Income that you are guaranteed not to outlive

5

GUARANTEED INCOME FOR LIFE

The idea of growing your retirement nest egg in a guaranteed (income account) wealth-building tool that will provide you with a guaranteed income for life that you can *never* outlive is absolutely amazing to most readers.

If you desire a guaranteed return on your retirement combined with a guaranteed income stream for life, then this chapter may be the most important chapter that you ever read.

How do you obtain a guaranteed return combined with a guaranteed income for life?

Life insurance companies offer these guarantees when an individual buys a fixed indexed annuity (FIA) with a guaranteed lifetime income benefit rider (GIBR). You must add the GIBR when you purchase the FIA. If you choose to add a GIBR to your FIA, the accounting & reporting is different than a FIA without a GIBR.

On the next page, we will look at income account value vs. cash account value.

INCOME ACCOUNT VALUE VS. CASH ACCOUNT VALUE

When a GIBR is combined with a FIA, the insurance company must account for the Income Account Value (IAV) in addition to the Cash Account Value (CAV).

In every annuity, the CAV is the money actually growing at market rates each year. The IAV is the amount that will increase at the guaranteed interest rate offered by the insurance company.

For example, if your FIA offered an 8% GIBR, the guaranteed interest rate would be calculated only on the IAV.

The IAV is not cash that you could walk away with. It is only used to calculate the guaranteed lifetime income payment.

	Income Account Value	Cash Account Value
Purchased FIA at age 50 Includes 10% premium bonus	$110,000	$110,000
Year 1 (age 51)	$118,800	$113,960
Year 2 (age 52)	$128,304	$117,379
Year 3 (age 53)	$138,568	$121,839
Year 4 (age 54)	$149,654	$126,956
Year 5 (age 55)	$161,626	$131,273
Year 6 (age 56)	$174,556	$137,968
Year 7 (age 57)	$188,521	$144,452
Year 8 (age 58)	$203,602	$150,086
Year 9 (age 59)	$219,891	$156,089
Year 10 (age 60)	$237,482	$160,304
Year 11 (age 61)	$256,480	$167,037
Year 12 (age 62)	$276,999	$176,558
Year 13 (age 63)	$299,159	$185,562
Year 14 (age 64)	$323,091	$194,469
Year 15 (age 65)	$348,939	$203,220

Below is an example that compares how the IAV and CAV grow over a fifteen year period. The FIA used in this example has a 10% premium bonus and includes a GIBR with a guaranteed interest rate of 8%. This initial premium is $100,000 at age 50. For the CAV, a random rate of return is used to reflect real world activity. The example does not take into account surrender charges, as it is intended to merely reflect the growth difference between the IAV and CAV.

The IAV grows at 8% and is much higher than the CAV at each year end. At age 65, this IAV would result in a monthly retirement income of $1,454 for life.

Another favorable characteristic of GIBRs is that you can usually activate them after the first anniversary of the annuity and *not* incur surrender charges.

Most insurance companies limit the time they allow the IAV to grow to 10 years. Some companies allow up to 20 years. These limits are because insurance companies must set aside cash reserves to guarantee the return. The longer the accumulation period, the more cash reserves the insurance company has to allocate.

With this in mind, *younger individuals should not add the GIBR to an FIA* if they would not be initiating the income stream by the end of the accumulation period.

The main reason individuals purchase FIAs with GIBRs is so they are assured that they will *never* outlive their retirement income, no matter what happens with the market or the economy as a whole.

Don't let all the numbers and examples used is this chapter confuse you. The GIBR on FIAs is very easy to understand. The benefits can be summarized with the following bullet points:

- Your retirement money will never decrease with stock market declines

- A guaranteed rate of return between 4-8%

- A guaranteed income for life that you can never outlive

- Access to your money at all times (surrender charge may apply)

- Cash Account Value passes to beneficiaries at your death

If these bullet points reflect characteristics that you want to include in your retirement wealth-building and preservation strategy, then you are a prime candidate for a fixed indexed annuity combined with a guaranteed lifetime income benefit rider.

This is the most powerful retirement wealth-building and preservation strategy in the market. It's mathematically calculated, and incorporates an income that is both adequate and sustainable based on guarantees.

The primary reason individuals purchase a FIA that includes a GIBR is so they are guaranteed to *never* run out of income, especially if they live a long life. This guarantee is very comforting, and as the illustrations show, the income amounts are great.

I am sure that many readers will have questions about how GIBRs work after reading this chapter. Please feel free to email me at

Larry@CompleteBenefitSolutionsLLC.com;

or you can also visit and submit a question through our website at

www.CompleteBenefitSolutionsLLC.com.

6

ADDITIONAL TOOLS FOR CONSIDERATION

In addition to the retirement and wealth building tools discussed in earlier chapters, here are a few additional concepts that might work well in your financial plan.

LIFE SETTLEMENTS

A life settlement is simply the purchase of an existing life insurance policy insuring the life of an elderly person at a discount to its face value. The purchaser obtains legal and beneficial ownership of the policy, including the premium obligation to keep the policy in force, and holds it until its maturity. Upon the policy's maturity, the purchaser receives the payoff of the benefits of the policy as their return on investment.

A life settlement transaction allows the purchaser to invest in an asset that:

- has an inherent value

- does not rely on future market conditions for appreciation

- provides the opportunity for superior returns without a parity of risks

- and is not directly correlated to business cycles, commodity prices or the performance of financial markets.

Of course, just with any investment, life settlements have their own set of risks. Currently, there is no established secondary market for life settlements, so they are viewed as an illiquid investment that should be purchased with funds you can afford to have locked up for a potentially long period of time. This risk is greatly reduced by only purchasing a fractional interest in a number of different life insurance policies which are all issued by highly rated life insurance companies.

Since these risks are not directly tied to market or economic conditions, life settlements are a great way to truly diversify your investment portfolio.

FLEXIBLE PREMIUM ANNUITY

These are annuities with no fixed schedule for payment of premiums. For example, premiums can be paid for 10 straight months, then not paid for the next 10 months, then paid every other month, or any combination thereof.

Flexible Premium Annuities (FPA) typically rely on a series of contributions throughout the accumulation period, but can accept a single premium or contribution. The flexibility of contributions is an often undervalued benefit of FPAs.

The multiple contributions to FPAs can be unscheduled and irregular. The FPA merely accumulates a cash value based on the amount and timing of the contributions

The value of flexibility to the investor is that they can better manage the accumulation in response to changing personal circumstances and market performance. FPAs have a low opportunity cost and normally have no contributions limits.

The flexible premium annuity is another concept that increases the impressive range of options for the annuity investor. Where your finances are concerned, you deserve choices and power. Flexible premium annuities give you just that — choices and power.

SINGLE PREMIUM WHOLE LIFE

The main benefit of life insurance is to leverage funds to create an estate that can provide for dependents or to leave something to charity. Single premium whole life (SPWL) is a type of life insurance in which a lump sum is paid into the policy in return for a death benefit that is guaranteed to remain paid-up until you die.

SPWL policies pay a fixed interest rate based on the insurance company's investment experience and current economic conditions.

With SPWL insurance, the cash invested builds up quickly because the policy is fully funded. The size of the death benefit depends on the amount invested and the age and health of the insured. For example, a 60-year old female might use a $25,000 single premium to provide a $50,000 income tax-free death benefit to her beneficiaries, whereas a 50-year old male's $100,000 single premium might give a $400,000 death benefit.

While the death benefit provides you with an effective means to provide for your dependents, you also need to consider unexpected expenses that can crop up in old age. SPWL policies can offer a solution to the expensive predicament of long-term care.

Some SPWL policies will give you tax-free access to the death benefit to pay for long-term care expenses. This helps protect your other assets from the potentially overwhelming cost of long-term care. The remaining death benefit will pass tax free to your beneficiaries.

These types of policies give you control over your investment, allowing access to the cash value for emergencies, retirement or other opportunities. One way to tap into the cash value is with a loan. You can generally take a loan up to 90% of the policy's cash surrender value. This will, of course, reduce the policy's cash surrender value and death benefit, but you have the option to repay the loan and re-establish the death benefit.

Contrary to the equity indexed universal life policies I discussed in chapter 3, your investments will grow *tax-deferred* inside the policy and you will pay taxes on the earnings if you withdraw or borrow from the policy. Additionally, there is a 10% IRS penalty on all gains withdrawn or borrowed before age 59½. However, your named beneficiaries will receive all the benefits tax-free and without the time delay and expense of probate.

If you have a lump sum of cash that you don't need right now and you want guaranteed life insurance protection for your family or your favorite charity, a single premium whole life insurance policy may be the ideal product for you.

CONCLUSIONS ON
RETIREMENT PRESERVATION

This book will not solve every individual's problems, but I am confident that readers who take the advice offered in the book will be at ease with their retirement strategy. Just knowing that your retirement nest egg will not decline when the market tanks and will lock in gains annually relaxes the mind of most individuals.

Typically when I have read financial books, I wanted to get in touch with the author to ask questions. Therefore, I am including my personal email:

Larry@CompleteBenefitSolutionsLLC.com.

Please feel free to email me your questions or thoughts, and I will do my best to accommodate your inquiries.

If you are motivated by the topics covered in this book, I would appreciate your feedback.Both positive feedback and constructive criticism will help me when I update this book.

Thank you for reading this book, and please visit

www.CompleteBeneftSolutionsLLC.com

for more information on Retirement Preservation.

ABOUT THE AUTHOR

Larry P. Stidman is an advisor to individuals and business leaders all over the country. He has over fifteen years of financial and insurance experience as a Certified Public Accountant and independent insurance professional.

Born and raised in Arkansas, Larry comes from a prominent family of educators. His mother is a retired elementary teacher and his father is one of the most successful high school football coaches in Arkansas.

In 1992, Larry joined a local CPA firm and in the fall of 1995 founded his own accounting firm. In 2000, the business portfolio was expanded to offer insurance products and additional financial services. To better exemplify the organization's philosophy, it was rebranded to Complete Benefit Solutions in July 2007. The primary purpose is still the dedication of serving our clients' needs by building customized financial and insurance packages to help them reach their goals.

To discuss any of these financial tools in more detail, you can email the author at Larry@CompleteBenefitSolutionsLLC.com or call his direct office at 501-622-2552. You can also visit the website at

www.CompleteBenefitSolutionsLLC.com

www.ingramcontent.com/pod-product-compliance
Lightning Source LLC
Chambersburg PA
CBHW051258170526
45165CB00004B/1757